A NATION
TORN APART

A NATION
TORN APART

edited by
Miriam Rinn

Cover illustration by Vince Natale.

Copyright © 2000 by Troll Communications L.L.C.

Printed in the United States of America.   ISBN 0-8167-6307-0

10 9 8 7 6 5 4 3 2 1

TABLE OF CONTENTS

Robert E. Lee

D ay after day, week after week, eight-year-old Robert Lee waited for letters from his father. Robert noticed that little else made his mother smile these days. There were money problems, she wasn't feeling well, and most of all, Mama and everyone else in the family missed Papa. Even four-year-old Catherine, who could hardly remember him, missed her father.

Henry Lee had gone away to live in the West Indies because he owed a large number of debts, and he was unable to pay them. If Mr. Lee had stayed home, the authorities would have thrown him into debtor's prison. In the early 19th century, that was the punishment for people who couldn't pay their debts.

Henry Lee had been in debtor's prison twice before. Each time, his family had to sell some property to pay his debts and have him released. This time, however, there was not enough property left to sell.

Robert often thought of that day in June 1813 when his father left. He had been only six years old then, but he could not forget the sight of his mother weeping as she waved a final farewell. Nor could he erase the picture of his father, standing at the rail of the ship as it sailed for the island of Barbados.

Life was confusing to young Robert Lee. Everyone knew that Papa had done some foolish and bad things, but Mama spoke of Mr. Lee only as a great hero of the American Revolution. Robert's brothers, Carter and Smith, told him that Papa had been Virginia's best governor. If only Robert could forget the bad things....

Robert Edward Lee was born on January 19, 1807, in a lovely mansion called Stratford. The huge house sat on a grand plantation in Westmoreland County, Virginia, and was furnished with the finest things money could buy. Often the doors had to be kept shut with chains, however, for that was the only way the Lees could keep out the bill collectors. Robert's father constantly spent more money than he had, and his irresponsibility eventually caused the family to lose their home.

When Robert was three years old, the Lee family moved to the town of Alexandria, Virginia. Stratford had originally been owned by Mr. Lee's first wife, and she left it to their son, Henry Lee, Jr., when she died. When Henry became old enough to take over management of the estate, he asked his untrustworthy father and his new family to leave.

There was another reason for the move to Alexandria. Charles Carter Lee, called Carter, was almost 12 years old. Ann Lee was ten years old. Sidney Smith Lee, called Smith, was eight years old. Mrs. Lee felt they should be in proper schools, with other children their own ages. Alexandria had good schools, and the Lees had many relatives there. It seemed a perfect place to settle.

Even after Mr. Lee left the country for good, the family stayed in Alexandria. It was a pleasant town, right across the Potomac River from the city of Washington, D.C. The town of Alexandria wasn't large, but it had everything a child like Robert could want. There were docks along the river, where ships came from ports all around the world.

The young boy liked to sit and watch the bales of tobacco and cotton being loaded onto the ships. Workers unloaded cloth, machinery, furniture, and all kinds of foreign-made goods. Robert also liked to listen to the sailors talking in different languages, and to see their unusual clothing.

There was much to do in Alexandria. On warm days, Robert went swimming in a little cove, just outside the town, and he ice-skated there on cold winter days. But as much as he liked Alexandria, Robert liked another place even more. He loved the estate called Shirley, situated on the James River. It was a huge property, spread over 25,000 acres of land. It had forests, landscaped lawns, streams and ponds, and large sections used for farming.

The plantations of Shirley produced corn, wheat, vegetables, cotton, and flax. Slaves harvested fruit from the plantation's orchards. Its streams and ponds were an endless source of fish, and its forests yielded deer, turkey, and other wild game.

There were long rows of chicken houses, pens filled with geese and ducks, and herds of cattle, dairy cows, horses, pigs, goats and sheep. Except for sugar, spices, coffee, machinery, and some clothing, everything the occupants of Shirley needed was produced on the sprawling plantation.

Shirley belonged to the Carter family. Mrs. Lee, who was a member of that family, was always welcome there, once Mr. Lee had escaped to Barbados. She and her children enjoyed these visits very much. Robert especially looked forward to playing with his cousins who either lived there or—like him—were visitors.

Robert spent many hours watching the blacksmith shoeing horses, the millers grinding grain into flour, the carpenters repairing and making furniture, and the many other craftspeople at work. There were also hundreds of slaves on the Virginia plantation. Some worked as house servants, some as mechanics, and some as farm laborers. With all the people at Shirley—family, friends, visitors, and slaves—the plantation was as busy as a small city.

Robert's mother had 22 brothers and sisters, each of whom had children. In fact, there were so many children in the family that the Carters ran two schools to educate all of them. The girls attended one family school at Shirley. The boys attended the other family school at Eastern View. Eastern View was the plantation in Fauquier County, owned by Elizabeth Carter Randolph, one of Mrs. Lee's sisters.

Until Robert entered the boys' school at the age of nine, he had not attended any other school, but he did know how to read, write, and do arithmetic. When he was little, Robert's mother was his teacher. After a while, her place was taken by the tutors who lived at Shirley. This kind of education was normal for the children of wealthy families in the South at that time. Virginia had no public schools, and while private schools existed, they were not for young children.

Even though there was no planned system of education, Robert, his brothers, sisters, and cousins were expected to be well-educated by the time they were adults. It was understood that they would acquire an education for the same reasons that they would learn to dance, to ride a horse, and to behave properly in company—because they were members of Virginia's ruling class.

Robert took easily to the life at Shirley, where his family spent more and more time. He was a quiet, thoughtful, and very bright boy. Whatever he set out to learn, he learned thoroughly. He soon became a fine horseman, marksman, and athlete. He was quite polite, and showed a knack for doing the right thing in adult company. He was so serious and proper, in fact, that some of his cousins teased him about it, but they understood that family problems caused Robert to be so sober.

Robert had a difficult childhood in a number of ways. There was his father's disgrace, which he heard adults discuss quite often, and his mother's money problems troubled him, too. Being at Shirley was wonderful, but it was like taking charity. The horses he rode weren't his, nor was the food he ate, the bed he slept in, or the slaves who waited on him.

Robert saw himself as a poor relation who had to earn his keep by being a perfect gentleman. He had to prove that the Lees were respectable, worthy people. It was as if, by his exemplary behavior, Robert hoped to blot out his father's bad reputation.

Robert attended Eastern View for close to two years, and he proved to be a fine student. He also was able to relax a bit. His aunt, Mrs. Randolph, was an easygoing person who encouraged the boys to laugh and have fun. Robert would always look back on his years at Eastern View as one of the happiest periods of his childhood.

In 1818, tragedy struck the family, and Robert returned to Alexandria. After years of exile, his father had finally sailed for home, and then died on the voyage from the West Indies. His death crushed Mrs. Lee, who had never stopped hoping that their family would be reunited.

Even though he was just 11 years old, Robert knew he had to be the man of the house. Carter was finishing his law studies at Harvard University, and Smith was about to begin a career in the United States Navy. Robert's sister, Ann, was in Philadelphia, receiving treatment for tuberculosis. Only his younger sister, Catherine, who was just seven, was at home.

Robert did not hesitate to take over adult responsibilities. He did the marketing, managed all the housekeeping, directed the servants, paid the bills, looked after the horses, and saw to everything else that needed to be done. Taking care of the house was only one of his concerns. He also accompanied his mother on daily carriage rides, read to her, told her jokes, and made sure she took her medicine every day.

Even at this young age, Robert was extremely well organized. With all his duties, he also found time for fun. Robert and one of his cousins, Cassius Lee, loved to hunt ducks and catch fish, and did so often. They also practiced boxing and fencing, which were sports popular with Virginia gentlemen of the time.

The street fairs that came to Alexandria were special delights for the boys. They saw puppet shows, booths with magicians, fortunetellers, and games of chance. Robert and Cassius never missed a fair when one came to town.

One of Robert's favorite activities was going to the horse markets. From the time he was very young, Robert E. Lee was a horse lover. Everything about horses interested him, and he was considered a fine judge of horses. Robert learned about horses by watching the sales at the market, by asking questions of the dealers, and through personal experience gained by riding and caring for horses. His relations didn't hesitate to ask the youngster's advice before buying an animal for racing or for pulling a carriage.

Years later, when Robert E. Lee was a military officer, his experience at the horse market proved extremely valuable. His horsemanship won him the respect and admiration of both officers and troops. Furthermore, Lee insisted that his army acquire the best horses, and he couldn't be fooled on the price or quality of the animals.

Perhaps the most important lesson Robert learned at the horse market was how to communicate with all kinds of people. While the grooms, traders, and blacksmiths at the market were not educated gentlemen, they were wise in the ways of their world. Young Robert learned from them and came to respect them. In turn, they responded to his friendship.

Lee's ability to get along with everyone served him well when he commanded Confederate troops in the Civil War. More than any other general of his time, Robert E. Lee inspired loyalty and love from his soldiers. Any soldier could approach the general with a problem or a complaint.

When Robert was 12, his mother enrolled him at the Alexandria Academy, on Washington Street. The schoolmaster, Mr.

William B. Leary, stressed Latin, Greek, and mathematics. Mr. Leary was glad to have Robert as a student, and the boy did well in all his subjects, especially in mathematics.

Robert attended the Alexandria Academy for three years, and during that time a special bond developed between him and Mr. Leary. In many ways the schoolmaster became a substitute for the father Robert did not have.

When Robert finished his studies at the academy, he faced a major decision: which career should he follow? He could not afford to live as a gentleman, and his mother could not afford to send him to college. This meant he would have to learn a trade or enter military service.

The idea of serving in the United States Army appealed to Robert. It was a chance for him to follow the path his father had taken as a military hero. "Light-Horse" Harry Lee was still honored for his glorious deeds during the American Revolution.

Robert also hoped to make a name for himself—a great name. He wanted to make Virginians forget the shame his father had brought to the Lees in his later years. More than anything, Robert wanted to be well respected in Virginia, his native state.

Late in 1823, 16-year-old Robert told his family he wanted to go into military service. They all approved wholeheartedly. In fact, at a gathering of the Lee clan, someone suggested that Robert ask for an appointment to the U.S. Military Academy at West Point, New York. There, he could get a free college education and train to be an officer.

With the excellent military reputation of his father and letters of recommendation from a number of important Virginians, Robert E. Lee was accepted by West Point in 1824, but he was told he would have to wait a year. There were so many applicants ahead of him that Robert could not be admitted until July 1, 1825.

Until that time arrived, Robert continued his studies at a school near the Lee home. It was run by a schoolmaster named

Benjamin Hallowell. Years later, Mr. Hallowell wrote, "Robert E. Lee entered my school in the winter of 1824-1825 to study mathematics, preparatory to his going to West Point. He was a most exemplary student in every respect. He was never behind time at his studies, never failed in a single recitation, was perfectly observant of the rules and regulations of the institution. He imparted a neatness and finish to everything he undertook. The same traits he exhibited at my school he carried with him to West Point."

Robert E. Lee entered West Point at the age of 18, and his 4 years there set standards that are still regarded with awe. Lee earned the distinction of never receiving a single demerit. In those days, the superintendent of the Academy kept a book with a page set aside for each cadet. On this page, all the demerits were entered as a permanent record. Lee's conduct was flawless, and his page did not have a mark on it. In fact, by his third year, his page was given to another cadet who was always in trouble. In addition to his perfect behavior, Lee was graduated second in his class academically.

After he was graduated in 1829, Second Lieutenant Robert E. Lee rushed home to Alexandria, where Mrs. Lee was gravely ill. She died soon after his return, and Robert took the death of his beloved mother very hard. His only consolation was that his success at West Point had made her happy.

In the 32 years between Lee's graduation and the beginning of the Civil War, he served at various Army posts. He was a captain in the Corps of Engineers in the Mexican War. He was superintendent of West Point from 1852 to 1855. After that tour of duty, Colonel Lee commanded the Department of Texas. This was before Texas became part of the Union.

Lee was nearing retirement when the nation was split apart in 1861 by the Civil War. That year, he was offered a high command in the fight against the South. Though he was a southerner,

Colonel Lee prepared to accept the offer. Before he could say yes, however, Virginia seceded from the Union to join the Confederacy.

Despite his personal aversion to slavery and the idea of secession, Robert E. Lee had always felt a deep sense of loyalty to Virginia. When his state seceded, he promptly resigned his commission in the U.S. Army. The deciding factor in his choice of service was the defense of his native state.

As a Confederate general, Robert E. Lee was a brilliant and well-loved commander, but not even his valiant leadership could change the war's outcome. The North had more troops and supplies, and it was only a matter of time before the South would be defeated. That time came on April 9, 1865, at the town of Appomattox Court House, Virginia. On that day, Robert E. Lee, commander-in-chief of all Confederate armies, signed the surrender and offered his sword to General Ulysses S. Grant, leader of the U.S. Army.

Intending to spend his remaining years quietly, Lee retired to his Virginia home, but he was immediately offered the presidency of Washington College (now called Washington and Lee University), in Lexington, Virginia. Concerned for the financial security of his family, he accepted and served in that capacity until his death on October 12, 1870. His passing was mourned in the North as much as the South, for the nation had lost a great man.

Abraham Lincoln

The sun was just starting to push its way over the horizon. Its golden light chased away the shadows of the woods around the cabin at Sinking Springs Farm. The air stayed chilly and cold the morning of February 12, 1809, as it almost always does during a Kentucky winter. It was nearly as cold inside the one-room log cabin, but the people in the room were too busy to care. Mr. Tom Lincoln sat on a chair in one corner, talking quietly to Sarah, his two-year-old daughter.

"Your mother will be just fine," he said. "You sit right here on pappy's lap and don't worry about a thing."

A few moments later, the loud wail of a baby was heard.

"It's a boy, Tom," Elizabeth Sparrow called out. Elizabeth, Mrs. Nancy Lincoln's aunt, had come to the cabin the day before to help with the birth.

The infant, named Abraham after his grandfather, had a strong voice. He was a large baby, sturdy and healthy looking. But he was very homely. At least, that was what nine-year-old Dennis Hanks thought. Dennis, the Sparrows' adopted son, came to see his new cousin as soon as the adults would let him into the cabin.

Dennis would always remember the day Abraham Lincoln was

born. When he entered the cabin, Dennis saw Nancy Lincoln lying in bed, looking tired, but very happy. Tom Lincoln threw a bearskin over Nancy to keep her warm, and then he built a great fire.

Betsy Sparrow was busy washing and dressing the new baby. When Dennis asked if he could hold little Abe, Nancy said, "Yes, but be careful," and handed him the squirming infant.

As soon as Abe was in his cousin's arms, he began to wail. The more Dennis tried to soothe him, the louder Abe cried. At last, Dennis handed the baby back to Mrs. Sparrow. "Take him!" Dennis said. "He'll never amount to much."

Sinking Springs Farm was Abe's home for the first two years of his life. Then Tom Lincoln got tired of trying to grow crops in poor, rocky soil and moved his family to a farm at Knob Creek, ten miles away. As soon as they got there, Mr. Lincoln, a skilled carpenter, set to work building a log cabin and furniture.

It was easier for the pioneers to make new furniture than to carry old furniture from one place to another. Once they settled in a new place, they had to cut down many trees to clear the land for farming. That gave them a great amount of wood to build a cabin, furniture, and fences, and still have plenty left over for firewood.

Like most pioneer children, Abe and Sarah helped with the chores. Once he was big enough, Abe cleaned ashes from the fireplace, filled the woodbox with dry branches that he collected in the forest, and hauled water from the creek. He did anything else his mother or father asked him to do, too. Sarah helped her mother tend the farm animals, do the cooking and baking, wash the clothes, and tidy the cabin.

Abe's earliest memories of childhood were of those days at Knob Creek. "I remember very well," he wrote, "our farm was composed of three fields. It lay in the valley surrounded by high hills and deep gorges. Sometimes when there came a big rain in the hills, the water would come down through the gorges and spread all over the farm…I remember one Saturday afternoon. We planted pumpkin and corn seeds in what we called the big field; it contained seven acres—and I dropped the pumpkin seed. I dropped two seeds every other hill and every other row. The next Sunday morning there came a big rain in the hills; it did not rain a drop in the valley, but the water coming down through the gorges washed ground, corn, pumpkin seeds, and all clear off the field."

Life was a struggle for frontier families like the Lincolns. They needed every bit of food they could grow to feed themselves through the year, and one long dry spell or one bad flood could destroy a whole year's crops. If that happened, it brought terrible hardship to the farm families. They barely stayed alive, eating berries and nuts from the forest, and any game they could hunt. It was tough enough to live this way in warm weather, but it could mean starving in the winter.

The flood that Abe never forgot didn't cause too much suffering because it came so early in the planting season. This gave the Lincolns enough time to plant another crop. So Abe and his father, along with Mr. Sparrow and Dennis Hanks, worked from morning till night, reseeding the field.

Life wasn't all work for little Abe. He spent lots of time exploring the woods, fishing in the creek, and hunting with his father and the dogs. There were many exciting things to do for a young boy growing up in Kentucky, but there was danger, too.

One Sunday, Abe was out playing with his best friend, Austin Gollaher. The boys wanted to cross Knob Creek to find some partridges they had spotted the day before. Rain had made the creek's waters deep and dangerous, but that didn't stop the boys.

There was only one way to cross the creek, and that was to walk across a log that stretched from one side to the other. Abe went first, and fell in halfway across. "Neither of us could swim," Austin recalled. "I got a long pole and held it out to Abe, who grabbed it. Then I pulled him ashore. He was almost dead, and I was badly scared." Austin rolled and pounded Abe. Then he shook him, until the water came pouring out of his mouth. Abe was finally all right, and the two friends sat on the creek bank, talking about Abe's narrow escape.

Nancy Hanks Lincoln knew there were many dangers in the forest, and she was strict with her little boy when she had to be. But most of the time she was sweet and gentle and loving. She wanted only the best for her children, and when a school was opened down the road, Abe and Sarah were enrolled.

Zachariah Riney's one-room schoolhouse was a two-mile walk from the Lincoln homestead. It was a log cabin with a dirt floor and rows of rough log desks and benches. Mr. Riney taught "reading, writing, and ciphering," and he kept order with a birch rod.

The pupils said their lessons out loud, even their arithmetic. It sounded noisy and confused, which is why this kind of school was called a "blab school." The children learned their ABC's, how to spell a few words, and how to do very simple arithmetic. Six-year-old Abe practiced his letters by writing with a charcoal stick on the flat side of a split log. He wanted to make the letters as well as Mr. Riney made them, so he practiced every chance he got, when he wasn't doing chores.

The school was not free, but the frontier people were too poor to pay for their children's schooling with money. Instead, some paid the teacher with a bushel of corn or potatoes or a smoked ham. Other parents paid with fur skins from animals they had trapped, a cord of firewood, or anything else the teacher was willing to take.

The Lincoln children did not attend Mr. Riney's school for very long. In 1816, when Abe was seven, the Lincolns decided to move from Kentucky to Indiana. In December of that year, with frost covering the ground, they left Knob Creek forever. They traveled northwest through forests, across the Ohio River, and into

Indiana. After a rough journey, they reached their new home in the wilderness at Pigeon Creek.

The first thing the Lincolns did was to build a shelter. With snow falling steadily, the whole family worked to put up a kind of shed called a half-faced camp. It had just three walls made of logs, and a roof of branches and bark. The fourth side was left open.

A blazing fire burned day and night at the open side. During the day, Mrs. Lincoln cooked over the flames. At night, the fire kept the family from freezing as they slept on their "beds"—piles of leaves. All their furniture had been left behind in Kentucky. Tom planned to make beds, tables, and chairs as soon as he had time to build a real cabin, but the very first thing Tom Lincoln had to do, before beginning the cabin, was to cut down some trees.

Abe worked alongside his father, but it took weeks for the father and son to chop down enough trees for a cabin. There were so many other things to do every day—keep the fire at the camp blazing, fetch water from the spring a mile away, clear the land of stumps and stones to ready it for spring planting, and hunt for game to eat.

The woods were filled with all kinds of wild game. There were deer, bears, wild turkeys, ducks, geese, squirrels, rabbits, and wild pigeons. Years later, Abe remembered the day he shot his first— and only—wild turkey. When he saw he had hit the bird, he felt like a real hunter—proud to bring good food to the table. But when he saw the dead bird fall to earth, he felt very sad. From that day on, Abe didn't want to be a hunter. He did not like the idea of killing, and this feeling stayed with him for the rest of his life.

The Lincolns' cabin was completed early that spring, and the family was glad to have a real home again. It was just one room, like their Knob Creek home had been, but with one big difference! Mr. Lincoln planned something special for the cabin at Pigeon Creek.

"I reckon you children are about ready to have a place to

yourselves," Tom Lincoln told Abe and Sarah. "I have an idea that I think you'll like."

"What is it?" Abe asked.

"I'm putting an open loft over part of the cabin," Mr. Lincoln said, "and I'm knocking some pegs in the wall so you can climb up there."

The children loved their sleeping loft. The first day, they found countless reasons to climb up and down their ladder of wooden pegs. When the first harvest was in, Nancy Lincoln made them new cornhusk beds, and Abe and Sarah thought their sleeping loft was the greatest room in the world!

In the fall of 1817, Tom and Betsy Sparrow and Dennis Hanks joined the Lincolns in Indiana, moving into the half-faced camp Tom had built. The Lincolns were very glad to have their relatives so close. It had been lonely without them, especially with the nearest neighbors miles away.

Their happiness didn't last long. In the summer of 1818, Tom and Betsy Sparrow fell ill with "milk sickness." It was caused by drinking milk from cows that had eaten poisonous plants. Nancy nursed her aunt and uncle, but without a doctor or medicine it was hopeless. The Sparrows died in September. Not long after, Nancy became ill, too, and died of the same sickness on October 5, 1818.

The world was suddenly a drab and lonely place for the Lincoln family. Sarah did her best to cook and clean, and Abe worked hard with his father and Dennis out in the fields, but the spirit had gone out of all of them. Their clothes grew ragged, and the house got dirtier and dirtier.

Then, in November 1819, Tom Lincoln took a trip back to Kentucky. He told the children to be good and take care of themselves till he got back. He rode off into the woods, promising to return as soon as he could.

It was a frightening time for the youngsters. At night they could hear bears and wildcats prowling in the dark woods near the cabin. During the day things were better. Dennis shot quail and rabbits for dinner. Abe and Sarah gathered nuts and berries in the woods. Abe also ground corn for Sarah to bake into pone cakes. It wasn't easy living this way, but it kept them from thinking too much about their fears and loneliness.

Then one sunny day in December, the children heard the sound of a wagon coming through the woods. They ran out of the house and saw Tom leading a team of four horses harnessed to a covered wagon.

"Say how-do to your new mother!" Tom shouted happily, as he helped a woman down from the wagon. She was tall and had a gentle smile. She came over to the Lincoln children and put her arms around them.

"I'm mighty pleased to meet you," Mrs. Sarah Lincoln said. "Now come and meet my children."

She led Abe, Sarah, and Dennis to the wagon. Standing there were two girls, 13-year-old Sarah Elizabeth and 10-year-old Matilda, and one boy, 9-year-old John. Now life at Pigeon Creek wouldn't be lonely anymore. They would be a real family again.

The second Mrs. Lincoln brought many changes to Pigeon Creek. First, she had Abe and John fill a trough with water. Then she bathed Abe and Sarah and told Dennis to scrub himself clean. After that she set about cleaning and washing and dusting the cabin. She had brought good furniture, pewter dishes, feather pillows and mattresses, pots and skillets, a flax wheel, and a soap kettle. All of these were left outside until she felt the house was clean enough for them. She asked Tom to put down a wooden floor and build a real door for the cabin, and she told the boys to whitewash the walls and ceiling.

"Now," she said, when everything was done, "we have a proper home!"

Right away, Abe liked his stepmother. She was a kind, intelligent woman, with a good sense of humor. She had brought something with her that interested Abe very much—books. Abe loved to read, and Mrs. Lincoln thought that was just fine.

Although Tom Lincoln would have liked Abe to forget about "book-learning" and get on with farming, his wife told him that Abe was going to be a great man someday and should be educated. Whenever the school near Pigeon Creek was open, she encouraged Abe to go.

Abe enjoyed school and did his work carefully and well. On one of his arithmetic notebooks, between neat rows of numbers, he wrote:

> Abraham Lincoln is my name
> And with my pen I wrote the same.
> I wrote in both haste and speed
> And left it here for fools to read.

The tall, skinny boy practiced writing every chance he got, and he was always reading or getting ready to read. Before setting out to plow the fields in the morning, Abe would put a book inside his shirt and fill his pockets with cornbread. When noon came, he'd sit down under a tree, reading and eating at the same time. In the house at night, he'd tilt a chair by the chimney and read.

About his passion for reading, Abe himself said, "The things I want to know are in books; my best friend is someone who'll give me a book I haven't read."

There was no library in his part of the world, and very few people owned books, but Abe tracked down the few books there were in that part of Indiana. Once he walked 20 miles to borrow a book about the history of the United States. Another time a neighbor lent him a biography of George Washington. That night, after he finished reading, Abe tucked the book into a corner of the loft. While he slept, there was a big storm, and rain stained the book cover. To pay for the damage, Abe spent three days harvesting corn for the farmer who had loaned him the book. Even as a youngster, and even when it meant doing hard work, Abe was ready to take responsibility for his deeds.

There were two books that meant a lot to the serious teenager. One was an Indiana law book. Abe read it over and over again, until he almost knew it by heart. He wanted to learn everything there was to know about the way laws worked, and how they could be used for the good of people. Years later, Abe would become a lawyer by reading every law book he could get his hands on, and working as a clerk for a lawyer in Illinois.

The second book that Abe read over and over had facts about geography, science, and world history. He learned things from this book that his friends and neighbors had never heard of.

Abe *was* different from his friends and neighbors, but he was still well liked. He was a great storyteller, and had a wonderful sense of humor. That was important to people in Pigeon Creek, where folks used to gather at the village store even when they had nothing to buy. They came to swap tales and gossip. That was one of their favorite ways of entertaining themselves.

Being a good storyteller was a matter of pride, and each person tried to outdo the others. Abe, who had been shy for a long time, "got the hang of talking" in front of the story-swappers at the village store. He learned so well that he was soon the best storyteller for miles around.

That teenage storyteller grew up to become one of the finest public speakers in American history. As a member of the Illinois assembly, as a young lawyer in his famous debates with Stephen Douglas, and as President of the United States, Abe's skill as a speaker won him respect and admiration. His speech memorializing the fallen Civil War soldiers at Gettysburg, Pennsylvania, is considered one of the great works of American literature.

The poor backwoods boy grew up loving people, the land,

and the law. One day he would prove his love for all these by serving as his nation's 16th president. He would lead his country through the worst days of the Civil War, free Americans who were trapped in slavery, and give new meaning to the word "liberty."

Harriet Beecher Stowe

Harriet's hands opened and closed nervously. It was almost time for her essay to be read. What would her father, the famous clergyman Dr. Lyman Beecher, think of his 12-year-old daughter's attempt? Harriet shivered with excitement and dread. Her essay on the immortality of the soul had been chosen to be read aloud at the closing exercises of the Litchfield Female Academy, but that didn't mean her father would approve. Harriet was too shy to participate in the lively discussions that went on around the Beecher dinner table. Her brilliant brothers and sisters argued back and forth about all sorts of things—religion, slavery, abolition—while she, the dull, quiet one, just sat and listened. In her last year at the academy, however, she had begun to show some talent for music and for writing. Perhaps her father would like what she wrote. He might even think she was as clever as her brothers.

"The sun of the Gospel has dispelled the darkness that has rested on objects beyond the tomb." The reader's voice rang out Harriet's words. She could see her father on the podium, his glance alert, attending closely. Then he leaned over to the principal, listened a moment, and turned to gaze at Harriet. Her heart almost burst with joy. He was proud of her! She could tell from his broad smile and slight nod.

Harriet's father was imposing enough to intimidate most people. Lyman Beecher had married Roxana Foote in 1799, after graduating from Yale Divinity School, and had accepted his first parish in East Hampton, New York. With the Beecher family growing, Lyman took an offer from a larger church, and the family moved to Litchfield, in northwest Connecticut. Litchfield was the county seat at the time, a busy and sophisticated town. Its courthouse and law school attracted lawyers and judges, and its merchants traded with Boston and New York. Lyman became acquainted with many respected and important men there.

In a short time, Dr. Beecher's fervent sermons were renowned not only in Litchfield, but all over the United States. A descendant of the first Puritans, he shared their strict, unyielding faith. He preached against dueling, against rival sects, and against the evils of alcohol.

Harriet Beecher was born on June 14, 1811, the seventh child in what had become one of the most influential families in the country. Like the other Beecher children, she would inherit her father's intensity and apply it to the great social issues of her time—slavery and women's rights.

By 1812, the Beecher house was crammed. In addition to Lyman and Roxana and their six living children, there was Roxana's sister Mary, two boarders, two indentured servants, Lyman's ward, and an abundance of cats and dogs. The house vibrated with the shouts and laughter of children, feet pounding up and down the stairs, and the constant activity that would always characterize the Beecher home. Only Aunt Mary kept to herself, groaning and weeping.

Little Harriet often wondered why Aunt Mary was so sad. All she knew was that her young aunt had left her husband in Jamaica. There were whispers about slaves and events too horrible to talk about. Harriet absorbed these whispered rumors and retrieved them much later when she wrote her stirring novels against slavery.

Although Lyman could terrify his parishioners with his depiction of a fiery hell, he was a fun-loving and devoted father. He described his temper as "quick and quick over." Harriet loved to play with her father and older brothers, William, Edward, and George. She was only sorry that she was so often excluded from their rough-and-tumble games. While the boys went exploring, she was told to sew a straight seam. Why was she not allowed to go fishing or hunting in the woods? Her sisters Catharine and Mary didn't seem to care, but Harriet did.

After she learned to read, she retreated to books. Reading could always take her someplace else, somewhere exciting and new. Harriet read *The Arabian Nights;* Shakespeare's magical play, "The Tempest"; and Cotton Mather's history of her own people, the Puritans. She loved the romantic novels of Sir Walter Scott and the poetry of Lord Byron.

When Harriet was only five years old, her mother died. Roxana had borne two more sons, Henry and Charles, before her death. Harriet loved her little brother Henry right away, and the two were devoted to each other for the rest of their lives. They resembled one another, each having heavy-lidded blue-gray eyes. When they were teenagers, Harriet and Henry switched clothes as a prank. Wearing his sister's hoop skirt, bonnet, and veil, Henry was a dead ringer for Harriet. Later, his flair for the dramatic would help Henry become as famous a preacher as his father, almost as famous as his favorite sister. In a world with no movies, radio, or television, traveling preachers who could hold audiences spellbound for hours at a time were as celebrated as rock stars.

A year after Roxana died, Lyman Beecher returned to his home from one of his many trips. "Here's Pa!" he announced to his excited children. "And here's Ma," said a voice from behind him. Harriet's father had remarried and brought his new wife

home as a surprise to his family. His children never warmed up to
their stepmother, Harriet Porter, but she came from a well-
established family in Maine and was a good wife to Lyman, bearing
him four more children.

In the early 19th century, there were not many choices for
women. They could marry and have families of their own, or they
could stay with their parents and care for them as they grew older.
The education most girls received prepared them for lives as wives
and mothers. The school Harriet attended, however, was different.
One of the first schools for girls in the United States, Sarah Pierce's
Litchfield Female Academy taught its students history, geography,
astronomy, and logic, as well as needlework and dancing. The
students at the all-girl school learned the same subjects that boys
did. That was a revolutionary concept.

It was at the Litchfield school that Harriet wrote her award-
winning essay. She soon wrote other pieces, including a drama in
iambic pentameter, the same meter Shakespeare used. Her play was
set in Rome and was about a careless young man who found peace
when he became a Christian. Although she was a fine writer,
Harriet was not the best student in her family. That honor
belonged to her sister Mary. Harriet was too easily distracted to
focus on subjects that bored her, such as arithmetic.

When Harriet finished her studies at Litchfield Academy, she
became a student at her older sister Catharine's school, the
Hartford Female Seminary. Like Sarah Pierce, Catharine believed
that girls needed a good education. Her students, who were all
teenagers, studied the same subjects Harriet had studied at the
Pierce school. Unlike Litchfield Academy, which had male teachers,
Catharine's school was run entirely by women. Catharine also used
student teachers, including her sister, to instruct the girls. While
Catharine traveled and wrote letters to raise money, Harriet stood
at the front of the classroom, teaching subjects that she herself had
just mastered.

Religion was central to the curriculum at the Hartford Female Seminary, as it was central in the Beecher home. Both Catharine and Harriet were deeply concerned about the spiritual life of their students. Christian beliefs would inspire Harriet's writing for the rest of her life, and convince her that slavery was not only wrong, but a sin.

When Lyman announced his intention to move to Cincinnati in 1832, both Catharine and Harriet decided to go along. Situated on the Ohio River, Cincinnati was a boomtown. In 1830, the population had been 25,000; by the time that Harriet would leave in 1850, it would have jumped to almost 114,000. The town was filled with merchants, craftsmen, and traders. Steamboats traveled the river, carrying goods to and from the "Queen City." So many hogs were driven to Cincinnati from the surrounding farms that it was also nicknamed "Porkopolis."

A commercial center, Cincinnati connected the eastern cities with the new western territories. It also stood between the North and the South, and different attitudes toward slavery were common. Although illegal in Ohio, slavery was legal in Kentucky, only a short boat ride away on the other side of the Ohio River. There were black men and women in Cincinnati who had escaped from their masters and were trying to make their way along the Underground Railroad to Canada and freedom. They could hide among the free blacks who lived in the city. Many Southerners could be found in Cincinnati too, including slave catchers on the trail of escaped slaves.

Upon arriving, Lyman became president of Lane Theological Seminary, and Catharine opened the Western Female Institute. Once more, Harriet worked in her sister's school. Teaching didn't excite her any more than it had back East, but she was writing again, and that was wonderful. Her first book, a geography for children, was published in 1833. It had Catharine's byline, but it was a great thrill for Harriet anyway, and it sold well. A year later, she won a writing contest and $50 with an entry entitled, "A New England Sketch." Fifty dollars was a lot of money, and this time her own name, Harriet Beecher, was on her work.

In 1836, Harriet married Calvin Stowe, who had been a student of her father's, in a small, private ceremony. They didn't need to find a clergyman to marry them, for, as Harriet said, there were plenty in the family. Besides Lyman, all her brothers had become ministers. The Stowes quickly started building their family, with the birth of twin girls. The babies kept coming, and by 1850, she had borne seven children.

Soon Harriet had to hire someone to help with the housekeeping. She felt lucky to find a young black woman, who had two young children. The woman and her children fit right into the Stowe household, and in between caring for her children and managing her household, Harriet found some time here and there to write.

One day, Harriet's servant came to her, trembling with fear. She had lied, she confessed to Harriet. She was not a free woman. She was an escaped slave from the South, and she had spotted her master in the streets of Cincinnati. He had come to capture her and her children, she was sure of it, and return them to slavery. Would Harriet help her?

Harriet stood, speechless. Of course she would help. She had always thought that slavery was the foul injustice that was staining the soul of all Americans. Now that she had seen it up close, she was more convinced than ever of its inherent evil. The idea that one person could own another was loathsome, and this terrified woman in front of her was proof of slavery's cruelty.

Harriet reassured the woman as best she could, and then she ran to Calvin's study. They remembered hearing about an Underground Railroad station on the outskirts of Cincinnati. They would hide the woman and her children in a wagon and drive them out to the station after night fell.

This experience stirred Harriet profoundly. In her mind she added it to other accounts she'd heard about slavery. Someone had told her the story of a slave mother who escaped across a frozen river, clutching her infant child. There was her own Aunt Mary, who had left her slave owner husband in Jamaica. Harriet filed them all away in her memory. Not many years later, she would draw on these memories to write her most famous book, *Uncle Tom's Cabin*.

Harriet loved her husband, but she realized soon after they married that he would not make very much money. Although a brilliant Bible scholar, Calvin had a retiring temperament and was often unwell. If they were to live comfortably, Harriet would have to earn money too. She began to write regularly for the Cincinnati newspapers. She wrote short pieces about New England, sketches of people she had known, stories for children, and helpful articles for women on how to manage a household. Soon, she was earning enough to hire regular household help.

In 1850, Calvin got a job teaching at a college in Maine, and the family settled into a new house. Back East, Harriet visited friends and relatives in Boston. Unlike Cincinnati, Boston was filled with abolitionist fervor. Abolitionists believed in the abolition, or immediate end, of slavery. The Fugitive Slave Act, passed in 1850, was causing panic among Boston's African Americans. Black people, many of whom were free, were being kidnapped and sent to the South. Her sister-in-law, a dedicated abolitionist, urged Harriet to write something that would awaken Americans to the horrors of slavery. Harriet, too, was an abolitionist, as was her brother Henry.

Sitting in church, Harriet suddenly had a vision of a man who was suffering deeply. Who was this man? In an instant she knew. He was a slave, and he had been cruelly mistreated. When she began to write down the vision she had seen, she felt as if she were possessed, as if someone else were guiding her pen. Later, Harriet told people that God had written *Uncle Tom's Cabin;* she had only put down the words.

The book was published in installments in a magazine called *The National Era*. The first installment appeared in June 1851, and it was an immediate sensation. When the story appeared in book form, 3,000 copies sold the first day. At the end of the second day, the entire first printing was gone.

Although Harriet wrote many other books, nothing had the impact of *Uncle Tom's Cabin*. It made her a celebrity in the United States and England. The book has never been out of print since its original publication, and it has inspired hundreds of thousands of people all over the world. In 1862, during the midst of the Civil War, Harriet supposedly had an interview with President Abraham Lincoln. The story was told that he greeted her with, "So you're the little woman who wrote the book that made this great war."

A more reliable testament to her influence was what happened in 1863. On New Year's Day in Boston's Music Hall, when the Emancipation Proclamation was read, immediately freeing all American slaves, the crowd stood up and chanted her name. To thousands of Americans, black and white, Harriet Beecher Stowe was the First Lady of Abolition.

Harriet Tubman

It was beautiful along the eastern shore of Maryland's Chesapeake Bay. The waters were filled with fish, oysters, and clams. In the woods lived rabbits, woodchucks, muskrats, deer, and squirrels. Corn, tobacco, wheat, and vegetables grew in the rich soil.

Maryland was a fine place to live during the early 1800s—if you were free. Ben Ross and Harriet Green were not. They were the slaves of a plantation owner named Edward Brodas. They worked in his fields, cut his lumber, and were his house servants. They did anything he ordered them to do, and their children did the same.

Slaves were called "chattel." That meant they were pieces of property, like sheep or furniture or bales of cotton. The slaves knew that they could be sold at any time. They knew that their children could be taken from them and sent far, far away, and that they could be beaten or whipped. They knew that their masters would never be punished, no matter what they did to their slaves, for slaves had no rights. They were not allowed any kind of education; they were not even allowed to attend church.

This was the sort of world into which Harriet Ross was born, around 1820. She was the sixth of 11 children born to Ben Ross and Harriet Green. They all lived in a tiny, one-room shack with a dirt floor, no windows, and no furniture. There were no beds, so the whole family slept on rags and straw spread on the floor. There were no dishes, so the slaves' food—mostly corn mush—was eaten right from the pot it was cooked in. They would scoop it out with a piece of flat stone or an oyster shell, standing or sitting on the hard ground.

Slave children had almost no time to play for they were put to work as soon as possible, to "earn their keep." When Harriet was still a very small child, she began running errands for Mr. Brodas and his family. She carried messages as far as ten miles away, walking over back roads, through woods, and along river banks.

The only tenderness in Harriet's life came from her family. They gave her so much love that she always had something wonderful to hold on to, even at the worst of times. One day— many years later—Harriet would thank her parents in the best way she could. She would rescue them, plus six of her brothers and one sister, from slavery, taking them north to freedom.

Soon after she turned five, Harriet was given a new task. Mrs. Brodas put her to work in the mansion, called the "big house." The little girl didn't know a thing about housework. She had never even been inside a real house before—only in the one-room slave shacks. To make things worse, nobody showed her how to do the things she was supposed to do in the mansion. It was no surprise that Harriet made all kinds of mistakes, and when she made mistakes, she was punished.

When Harriet was six, she was sent to live with a family of weavers named Cook, who lived many miles from the Brodas plantation. Harriet hated being so far from her family, but the Brodases wanted her to learn weaving. So, like it or not, Harriet went.

Life with the Cooks was no better than it had been on the Brodas plantation, but Harriet did not stay with the Cooks long.

One day, even though she was very sick with measles, Mr. Cook sent her down to the river. She was told to check his muskrat traps. To do this, she had to wade through ice-cold, fast-flowing waters.

The next day Harriet began to shake and cough. Soon she was burning with fever and could not do any work. Word of her illness quickly passed from one slave to the next, until it reached Harriet's mother. She ran to her master and begged him to bring her little girl home. Mr. Brodas agreed, for he didn't want to pay the Cooks for teaching someone who was too sick to learn. He had Harriet brought home, where her mother nursed the little girl back to health.

Harriet's next job was looking after Mrs. Brodas's baby. Years later, Harriet said, "I was only seven years old when I was sent to take care of the baby. I was so little I had to sit on the floor and have the baby put in my lap. And that baby was always in my lap except when it was asleep or its mother was feeding it."

Handling such a big responsibility was hard for young Harriet. She never had any time to play or be by herself. She was constantly watched by Mr. and Mrs. Brodas, and they were very strict with her. If she misbehaved, Harriet knew she would be given a whipping. This kind of punishment was used all the time, for the owners wanted to keep their slaves frightened. They were afraid that slaves would band together to speak up or fight back—or try to escape.

The slave owners failed in their attempt to break the spirit of all slaves. There always were slaves who stood up for their rights as human beings. They held religious services, even though that was forbidden. They studied reading and writing in secret. They hid and fed other slaves who were trying to escape to the North.

Every year there were slave uprisings. The plantation owners tried to keep the news of these revolts from getting out, for they didn't want their own slaves to hear of them. But word still passed from one slave to another, from one plantation to another all over the South. It didn't matter that the owners told each other—and the rest of the world—that the slaves were content; the slaves knew better.

From the time she was a baby, Harriet listened to the stories of slaves fighting back. She heard of a slave named Gabriel Prosser, who had planned a great rebellion in 1800. More than one thousand slaves were ready to march with him, but he was stopped at the last moment, when a traitor told several slave owners about the uprising.

Harriet also heard of Denmark Vesey, who preached that all people were equal. Vesey was a free black man who had once been a slave, and the leader of thousands of slaves living in South Carolina. In June of 1822, Vesey's group was ready to rise up in the name of freedom, but his plans, like those of Gabriel Prosser, were leaked to slave owners by frightened servants.

Harriet heard of other uprisings—large and small—taking place in many parts of the South. All this meant one thing to the young girl—she was not the only angry slave in America. *Someday, she told herself, I'm going to be free! And when that day comes, I'm going to help bring others to freedom.*

Harriet did not hide her feelings. She spoke out fearlessly to the other slaves on the plantation, and she refused to smile or make believe she was happy in front of the Brodas family. Harriet's mother worried about her. If Harriet angered her master or his wife, they might sell Harriet "down the river." Selling someone down the river meant selling that person to a slave trader. The trader would take his new slave down to the Deep South to be put to work in the rice or cotton fields. Life was hard for a slave in Maryland, but it was ten times harder in the Deep South.

Mrs. Brodas did not like Harriet's proud, defiant looks. She decided to break the child's spirit, and hired out the nine-year-old girl to another family in the county. These people made her work all day, cleaning house, and all night, caring for a baby. For no reason, she was punished every day, and she was fed only enough to keep her alive.

After a while, Harriet was little more than skin and bones. She was not able to work anymore. Now, sure that she was "broken," the family sent Harriet back to the Brodas plantation. Harriet's body *was* weak and wary, but her spirit was still strong.

Harriet's parents did their best to help her get well. Her mother nursed her every free moment she had, and her father taught her all kinds of amazing and useful things. Even though he had never gone to school, Ben Ross was a very wise man. He knew a lot about nature. He could tell that it would be a hard winter when the animals grew thicker coats in the fall, he knew where the fishing was good, and he knew which wild plants were safe to eat. As soon as Harriet was up and about, he took her on Sunday-afternoon walks in the woods and along the river.

Part of Harriet's strength came from her brothers and sisters. After a day of working in the fields under a broiling sun, they came back to the shack. They brought her all the news of the day. They sang songs, told stories, repeated jokes to make the little girl laugh. They did everything they could to make their sister happy.

Another part of Harriet's strength came from her faith. The slaves were not allowed to have a real church, but they were very religious and held services every Sunday morning. On every plantation there usually was at least one slave who could read or knew the Bible well. From this person all the other slaves learned Bible stories and prayers.

Of all the stories in the Bible, the one that held the most meaning for the slaves was about Moses, the Hebrew prophet who led his people out of slavery in Egypt. The American slaves prayed for a Moses of their own, someone who would lead them to freedom, too.

Harriet believed deeply that the burden on her people would

be eased, that they were meant to be free. She believed what the Bible said: that all people were equal in the eyes of God.

In the next three years, Harriet grew stronger in body and faith. As soon as she was completely well, Mr. Brodas hired her out to another master. This one had her do work hard enough for a grown man. She split rails with an ax, hauled wood, and did other heavy jobs. It was difficult, but she never gave up, even when it seemed too much to bear.

By the time she was 11, Harriet was muscular and very strong. She could work as hard and as long as any grown-up. Mr. Brodas saw this and put her to work in the fields. Like all the other women in the fields, Harriet wore a bandanna—a large handkerchief—on her head. For the rest of her life she would always wear a bandanna. It was to remind her of her days as a slave, and how far from the fields she had come.

In the summer of 1831, a slave from Virginia named Nat Turner led about seventy slaves in a bloody revolt. It took armed troops to stop the rebellion and three full months to capture Turner. Slave owners were frightened. If a revolt could happen in Virginia, it could happen anywhere. Haunted by fear, they tightened their hold on the slaves even more. Slaves were not allowed to gather in groups; they were not supposed to talk while they worked; they were never to be on the public roads without a pass from their masters.

No matter what the slave owners did, they could not extinguish the flame of freedom lit by Nat Turner. "I feel just like Nat Turner did," Harriet said one night to her family. "It's better to be dead than a slave."

"It's better to be alive and free," said her brother William.

"And how do we get that?" Harriet asked him. "You know Mr. Brodas won't ever give us our freedom."

"I'm not talking about what he gives," William told her. "I'm talking about what we take for ourselves—like a ride to freedom on the Underground Railroad."

"What's that?" Harriet wanted to know.

William told Harriet the story of Tice Davids. Mr. Davids was a slave in Kentucky who ran away. When the plantation owner found out that Davids was gone, he set out after him. Davids swam across the Ohio River with the owner rowing close behind, but by the time the owner's boat landed, there was no trace of Tice Davids. It was as if he had vanished into thin air.

The escaped slave had been helped by people who hated slavery, but the slave owner knew only that he had vanished. When the man returned home, he told everybody that "Tice Davids disappeared so fast, he must have gone on an underground road."

This story was repeated again and again. Of course, there was no underground road or tunnel from the South to the North, but the slaves kept telling the story anyway. Around this time, the first railroads were being built in the United States. Trains were the fastest way of traveling that anyone had ever seen. The slaves heard about the railroads, and soon people were talking about the "Underground Railroad" that took escaped slaves quickly and safely to the North.

The truth had nothing to do with trains and underground tunnels. The truth was that there were people who risked their lives to help slaves escape. Some of them hid runaways in their cellars, barns, attics, or in secret rooms in their houses.

These brave people were called "stationmasters." The hiding places were called "depots" or "stations." Other people took the runaways from one depot to another in a hay wagon, on horseback, or on foot. These people were called "conductors." The runaways themselves were known as "passengers" or "parcels." A child was a "small parcel," and a grown-up was a "large parcel."

After William told Harriet about the Underground Railroad, she thought about it all the time. *Maybe,* she told herself, *I'll take that ride to freedom. Maybe all of us will.* It was this hope that kept Harriet going.

When Harriet was 15, her hope—and her life—almost ended. One September evening she was sent to the village store. While she was there, another slave who belonged to a farmer named Barrett hurried in. A moment later, Mr. Barrett rushed in.

"Get back to the field!" Barrett shouted at the slave. The slave just stared back silently. Nobody else in the store made a move.

"I'll whip you," Barrett threatened. The slave began to edge away. "Stop!" Barrett yelled. "You," he said, pointing at Harriet and a young boy next to her. "Hold him so I can tie him up."

Harriet didn't obey, and she kept the boy from doing anything also.

Suddenly, the slave ran to the door. Barrett leaped to the store counter and picked up a heavy lead weight. He whirled and threw the weight at the runaway, but it missed its target. Instead, the heavy piece of metal struck Harriet in the head. She fell to the floor, unconscious.

For the next couple of months Harriet lay near death. At first, she couldn't eat. She grew thinner and thinner and slept most of the time. Her wound was healing slowly, but there was a very deep cut in her forehead. It left a scar she would carry for the rest of her life.

Mr. Brodas was sure Harriet was going to die, so he tried to sell her. Time after time he brought slave buyers to the shack, where Harriet lay on a pile of rags. Each time the buyer's answer was the same: "Even if she lives, she'll never be able to put in a day's work. I wouldn't give you a penny for her."

Winter came, and Harriet was still alive. Her parents were thankful, but they were still worried. Harriet could walk and talk and do light chores around the shack, but sometimes, in the middle of whatever she was doing, she fell asleep.

It could happen even while she was saying something. She would simply stop talking, close her eyes, and sleep for a few minutes. Then she would wake up and go on talking, as if no time had passed.

The Brodas family was sure that Harriet's "spells" meant her brain had been damaged, so they tried that much harder to sell her. Harriet did not want to be sold and sent away from her family, and her brain had not suffered any damage. On the contrary, she was a very clever 15-year-old. Every time Mr. Brodas came to the shack with a buyer, Harriet made believe that she was having one of her spells, or she acted very stupid. Her family and friends went along with Harriet's pretense, and the result was that no one was ever interested in buying her.

In time, Harriet's strength returned. She could lift huge, heavy barrels and pull a loaded wagon for miles. She drove the oxen in the fields and plowed from morning to night. It was said that she was stronger than the strongest man in Maryland. It was a strength she would need in the days to come.

Harriet's dream of freedom was still alive, but she put it off for a while. In 1844, she married a free black man named John Tubman. She hoped that he would help her get away to the North, but the marriage was not happy, and the two soon parted. Harriet continued to use the name of Tubman, however.

Not long after that, word reached the Brodas slaves that many of them were going to be sold. Harriet knew the time had come to make the break for freedom, so she turned for help to a white woman who lived nearby. This woman had once told Harriet, "If you ever need anything, come to me." Harriet knew that meant helping her to escape.

Without telling anyone, Harriet set out for Bucktown, where the white woman lived. When she reached the house, Harriet said to the woman, "You told me to come when I needed your help. I need it now."

The woman gave Harriet a paper with two names on it, and directions how she might get to the first house where she would receive aid. When Harriet reached this first house, she showed the woman there the paper. Harriet was told to take a broom and sweep the yard, so no one would suspect her of being a runaway. The woman's husband, who was a farmer, came home in the early evening. In the dark he loaded a wagon, put Harriet in it, well covered, and drove to the outskirts of another town. He told her to get out and directed her to a second "station."

Harriet was passed along this way, from station to station. She was riding the Underground Railroad, and she didn't stop until she crossed into Pennsylvania. Now she was free at last! As she remembered years later, "When I found I had crossed that line, I looked at my hands to see if I was the same person. There was such a glory over everything. The sun came like gold through the trees, and over the fields, and I felt like I was in Heaven."

But Harriet's "heaven" wasn't perfect. "I was free," she said, "but there was no one to welcome me to the land of freedom. I was a stranger in a strange land. And my home, after all, was down in Maryland, because my father, my mother, my brothers, my sisters, and friends were there. But I was free, and they should be free! I would make a home in the North and bring them there."

In the next few years, Harriet did what she swore she would do. She made trip after trip to the South, risking her life to bring others to freedom. She rescued her family, friends, other slaves— more than 300 men, women, and children. Harriet was beloved by the slaves, who called her their "Moses," because she led them through the wilderness and out of bondage, and hated by the slave owners, who offered a $40,000 reward for her capture.

Harriet was never caught. She became the most famous conductor on the Underground Railroad. As she said, "I never ran my train off the track, and I never lost a passenger."

The legend of Harriet Tubman grew during the Civil War. Fighting for the Union, she made many raids behind enemy lines as a scout and a spy, and as a nurse, she helped the sick and wounded soldiers, both Northerners and Southerners.

After the Civil War, Harriet made her home in Auburn, New

York. She never stopped doing good works. Until her death, on March 10, 1913, the woman called Moses fought for the right of women to vote, helped create schools for black students, and did everything she could for the poor, the old, and the helpless. When Harriet Tubman died, at the age of 93, she was honored with a military funeral. It was a fitting tribute to the woman who fought so many battles for the freedom of her people.

Frederick Douglass

Fred Bailey's world was bleak and poor, but the little boy didn't know it. Betsey and Isaac Bailey, his grandparents, were kind and loving people, and they took good care of Fred and his young cousins.

The children lived with Grandmama and Grandpapa because their mothers were not allowed to keep them. Their mothers—Grandmama Bailey's daughters—were slaves who worked on different plantations on the eastern shore of Maryland. When one of them had a baby, Grandmama Bailey took it in. She raised the child until it was old enough to be put to work by the slave owner.

Fred, who was born about 1817, was better off than a lot of other slave children. Many of them had no relatives like Grandmama Bailey to care for them. Those children were raised by strangers, who might not treat them well. Fred's grandmother made sure that her little ones had enough food and plenty of affection, and that they never felt lonely or frightened.

Betsey Bailey was smart and skilled in many ways. One of her special talents was farming. Her sweet potatoes grew bigger and better—and there were more of them—than anyone else's in the whole area. The neighbors said she was "born to good luck."

Grandmama's secret wasn't luck, Fred wrote years later. It was the special care and attention she gave to her seedlings.

To keep her sweet-potato seedlings from being destroyed by frost, she actually buried the roots under the hearth of her cabin during the winter months. Then, when they were planted, they were healthy and grew well. Whenever the neighbors had seedlings to put in the ground, they sent for Grandmama Betsey. "If she but touches them at planting," the neighbors believed, "they will be sure to grow and flourish." For lending her magic touch, Mrs. Bailey was always given a share of the crop, and that brought more food into the Bailey cabin.

For the first few years of his life, Fred never saw his mother. He didn't even *know* what a mother was. As for his father—the idea of such a person never entered his mind. If Fred belonged to anyone, it was to his master.

Little Fred spent his days playing with his cousins, helping his grandmother, or fishing in the river near the cabin. His only clothing was a rough, knee-length shirt. A slave child was given two shirts each year. Even if these shirts were torn or lost, there were no new ones until the year was up. Long after, Fred remembered, "In the hottest summer and the coldest winter, I was kept almost naked. No shoes, no stockings, no jacket, no trousers. Nothing but the coarse shirt reaching down to my knees. This I wore night and day, changing it once a week."

Until he was around five years old, Fred didn't know he was a slave. Then he heard his grandparents talking about the "Old Master," who owned all of Fred's family. There was a sad note in Grandmama Betsey's voice when she spoke about the plantation, where Fred would soon have to go. The little boy didn't understand much of what they were saying, but the sound of it made him shiver.

Nothing happened for two years. Then, one summer morning, Betsey Bailey took her grandson's hand and set off along the road. She didn't tell him where they were going, or why. She didn't cry or show any of the gloom she was feeling. Not once on the 12-mile walk to the plantation house did she speak one sad word. Yet somehow, Fred sensed that something terrible was happening.

In the blazing afternoon heat, Mrs. Bailey and Fred reached the plantation. The little boy saw many houses, farm animals, men, women, and children. All of this stunned him. Living at Grandmama's, he had never seen so many buildings and people all in one place.

Mrs. Bailey brought Fred over to a young boy and two young girls. "Fred," she said, "here is your brother, Perry. And these are your sisters, Sarah and Eliza. You run along and play with them. I'll sit in the kitchen and visit awhile."

Fred was confused and trembling. The children might be called brother and sisters, but they were strangers to him. He clung tightly to Grandmama's skirt. He wanted to go home.

Grandmama insisted that Fred stay outside and play. She gave him a gentle push toward the other children, then she walked away. Fred stood there, watching the other children play. Time passed, but he didn't budge from the spot. Then a child ran over to him, saying, "Your grandmammy's gone." Fred couldn't believe it. He dashed into the house to see for himself. It *was* true! Grandmama Betsey was gone.

The heartbroken boy threw himself on the floor and sobbed. His brother and sisters tried to comfort him, but nothing could stop his tears. Fred felt betrayed, terrified, and all alone. Now he suddenly understood what his grandparents had been talking about and why they had been so sad. Lying on the dirt floor, Fred cried himself to sleep.

For the next two years, Fred lived on the plantation as the slave of a man named Captain Anthony. Fred was still too young to work in the fields, so he was given other chores. He helped the older boys bring in the cows for milking. He kept the front yard clean. He ran errands for Captain Anthony's family.

Even though the work wasn't too difficult, Fred was always hungry and tired. Slaves were awakened long before sunrise and kept busy until long after dark. Breakfast for the slave children was cornmeal mush. It was dumped into a large wooden bowl on the ground. All the children squatted around the bowl to eat, scooping up the mush with oyster shells, flat stones, or their fingers.

The strongest children and the fastest eaters got the most food, but *nobody* ever had enough food. Little Fred got the least of all because Aunt Katy, the cook, was his enemy. One morning, Katy threatened to starve the life out of Fred. All day, he tried to keep up his spirits, hoping she would forget by dinnertime. But she didn't. At sundown, she gave each of the children dinner—one slice of corn bread. When Fred reached for his, she pulled away the loaf and sent him out of the kitchen.

The eight-year-old boy, too hungry to fall asleep that night, was sitting outside the kitchen door when he had a surprise visitor, his mother. Harriet Bailey was almost a stranger to Fred. Since he had come to the plantation, he had seen her only three times.

Fred's mother was a slave on a farm 15 miles away. The only way she could visit her children was to walk 30 miles at night. Her long, hard day in the fields left her too tired for that kind of walk. This time, however, she was able to get a ride on a cart.

Harriet Bailey put her arm around Fred and asked him how he was. He told her he was hungry and that the cook had threatened to starve him to death. The woman kissed her son, stroked his cheek, and said, "I won't let anyone starve you!" Then she gave him a heart-shaped ginger cake coated with sugar.

As soon as Fred finished the last crumb, his mother took him into the kitchen. In a voice filled with fury, she told Aunt Katy, "You're a slave just like the rest of us. How can you do these things to a harmless little child?"

Harriet Bailey's angry words didn't change Katy's treatment of Fred, but his mother's visit still made a big difference in the young boy's life. "That night," he remembered, "I learned that I was not only a child, but *somebody's* child." He knew that his mother loved him very much, and even though she couldn't be with him, she thought of him all the time. But after that night, Fred never saw Harriet Bailey again. She died when Fred was only eight or nine years old.

Before he was ten years old, Fred was sent to the city of Baltimore. He was going to work for Sophia and Hugh Auld, relatives of Captain Anthony. The young boy was glad to leave the plantation. He felt that whatever lay ahead could not be worse.

On a sunny Saturday morning in spring, Fred was dressed in a clean shirt and his first pair of pants. He was put aboard a sloop bound for Baltimore—a trip he never forgot. He gaped at the broad Chesapeake Bay and all the boats sailing on it. He marveled at the town of Annapolis, with its beautiful houses and the great shining dome of the State House. Most exciting of all was Baltimore itself, a city teeming with life. For the youngster who had never been away from the country, this was a fantasyland.

One of the sailors took Fred to the Auld house. Fred was met at the door by Mr. and Mrs. Auld and their little son, Tommy. Fred knew he was going to live with them and take care of Tommy. He didn't know how he was going to be treated, but when little Tommy smiled and took his hand, the young slave could see that fate had been kind to him.

Instead of sleeping on the ground, Fred now slept indoors on a bed of straw. He had clean clothes and enough food to fill his belly. Nobody beat him, and Mrs. Auld treated him like an ordinary child instead of a slave.

Every afternoon, when Fred brought Tommy home from play, the boys joined Mrs. Auld in the front parlor. There they sat quietly, listening to her read from the Bible.

Fred loved to hear Mrs. Auld read aloud. He enjoyed the sounds of the words and the wonderful stories they made. He wished he could read them, too. One day, he asked Mrs. Auld if she would teach him to read. "Why, how nice, Fred," she said. "It's delightful that you want to read the Bible. Of course, I'll teach you. We shall start with the alphabet this very afternoon!"

In the days that followed, Mrs. Auld gave Fred a reading lesson every afternoon. Soon the young slave knew the alphabet and could spell many short words. Fred looked forward to each afternoon's lesson with great excitement and was very proud when Mrs. Auld praised him for being so bright. He had never known such joy.

One evening, Mrs. Auld told her husband how well Fred was learning to read. Mr. Auld scowled. "You must stop these lessons right now!" he told his wife. "Don't you know that it is against the law to teach slaves to read? It's a bad thing to do."

"I didn't know it was against the law," Mrs. Auld answered. "And I cannot understand why it would be bad for a slave to read."

"A slave should know nothing but the will of his master," Mr. Auld explained. "If you teach that boy how to read, he'll be forever unfit for the duties of a slave. The knowledge will do him no good, and it will do us a great deal of harm."

Mrs. Auld never gave Fred another lesson. In fact, she did everything possible to stop him from learning. If she saw the boy looking at a newspaper or book, she snatched it away. If she didn't see or hear him doing some task, she accused him of sneaking off somewhere to read.

Life changed for Mrs. Auld, too. She was obeying the law and her husband and being a good slave owner, but she was no longer a happy woman.

Fred was hurt deeply by what had happened, but he learned two valuable lessons. First, he realized that his owners wanted him to be a slave forever. He understood now that people were not slaves because of something they did. They were slaves because somebody else wanted them to be.

The second lesson was that the way out of slavery was through knowledge. That was why slave owners kept their slaves ignorant. Once slaves could read road signs, they might run away from their masters. Once they found out that there were states without slavery, they might try to reach them. Once they learned to write, they could forge the papers slaves needed to travel. Once they could count, they could use money to buy train tickets and food.

Young Fred Bailey made up his mind to learn how to read and write. First, he read everything he could from a spelling book someone had thrown away. Whenever he came to a word he didn't know, he made a small mark under it and asked one of the neighborhood children to tell him what it was. Fred paid for these brief lessons with cookies from the Auld kitchen. By the time he was 13, Fred could read very well.

About the same time, Fred began working in the shipyard owned by Mr. Auld. His job was to clean up, watch the yard when nobody else was around, and keep the office fire going. There were many hours when he was alone, and Fred used them to teach himself to write.

One day, he found a school notebook Tommy Auld had finished using. In the spaces between the lines, Fred copied Tommy's writing. He worked in the kitchen by firelight, waiting until the Auld family was fast asleep.

Then in March 1833, Fred was sent back to the plantation. There had been a big argument in the Auld family between Hugh Auld and his brother, Thomas, and as a result, Hugh had to return Fred to the country.

Thomas Auld, Fred's new master, treated his slaves badly. Yet, no matter how many hardships he had to endure, Fred refused to beg or weep or show any other sign that it bothered him. This

made Thomas Auld so furious that he sent Fred away to be
"broken."

On January 1, 1834, Fred was brought to the farm of Edward
Covey. For a fee, Covey promised that he would turn "trouble-
making" slaves into obedient workers. For the first six months,
Fred took everything Covey handed out, but finally one day, when
Covey was beating Fred, the 17-year-old slave fought back. Fred
won the fight, knocking Covey to the ground. The enraged slave
breaker swore he would kill Fred, but the teenager knew better.
Covey would not do anything that would cost him his fee.

From that moment until Fred left Covey's, the young slave
was never whipped, nor did Covey ever again challenge him. Years
later, Fred wrote, "This battle with Mr. Covey was the turning
point in my life as a slave. It rekindled in me the smoldering
embers of liberty. I was a changed being after that fight. I was
nothing before; *I was a man now*. It inspired me with a renewed
determination to be *a free man*!"

After three years of farm work, Fred was sent back to
Baltimore. There, Hugh Auld got him a job in a friend's shipyard.
Fred liked the work—he was a skilled laborer now—and he was
happier in Baltimore than he had been in the country, but there
was one important thing still missing—his freedom! Then he met a
man who offered him a way to escape slavery.

The man was a black sailor who had seaman's papers. These
papers, issued by the United States government, proved that the
sailor was not a slave. With them, he was free to travel anywhere in
the country. The sailor offered to lend Fred his papers. "Put these
in your pocket," he said, "and you can go North to freedom. You
can mail them back to me when you're safe in New York or
Boston."

On September 3, 1838, wearing sailor's clothing and carrying
his friend's papers, Fred Bailey got on a northbound train. He
didn't stop until he reached New Bedford, Massachusetts, a

shipbuilding town. There, Fred took a job in a shipyard, married Anna Murray, a free black woman from Baltimore, and started a new life.

It was in New Bedford that Fred took the last name of Douglass. As Fred Bailey, he might be traced by bounty hunters who were paid for turning in runaway slaves. With a new name, Frederick Douglass, he had a much better chance of staying free.

It was also in New Bedford that Fred began the career that would make him world famous. He started by joining a group of abolitionists, people devoted to ending slavery. He read everything he could about slavery and listened to the leading abolitionists of his day. Then, in 1841, Frederick Douglass made his first anti-slavery speech. It thrilled his audience, and it brought him to the attention of every important person in the abolitionist movement.

For the next four years, Frederick Douglass toured the Northern states, speaking against slavery. He also wrote the story of his life. The book, which described his years as a slave, was read all over the United States. It was even read by the Auld family, who grew very angry. They went to court to have their runaway slave returned to them.

Douglass's friends were afraid that he would be arrested and sent back to Maryland, so they put him on a ship bound for England. In the two years he spent in England, he became a very popular speaker and writer. Douglass wanted to come home, however, where he felt a strong voice against slavery was needed more than ever. To make this possible, his friends raised enough money to buy his freedom from the Aulds.

When he returned to the United States in the years before the Civil War, Frederick Douglass continued his work for freedom. He started a weekly newspaper in Rochester, New York, called *The North Star,* which soon became a leading force in the battle against slavery.

Shortly after the war began, Douglass went to see President

Abraham Lincoln. He urged the President to recruit black men, as well as white, into the Union Army. "Why do you fight the rebels with only one hand," Douglass asked, "when you might strike effectively with two?"

Lincoln agreed. Within months, thousands of black men were fighting for the Union. Among them were two of Frederick Douglass's sons.

Even though the Civil War ended slavery, many problems remained for black people, and they still did not have equal rights. In many places, they could not vote, hold public office, find jobs, or get an education. Douglass continued his battle for civil rights and freedom. He fought tirelessly for an end to job discrimination and to the segregation in schools and places of worship.

Frederick Douglass did not stop fighting until his death on February 20, 1895. Even though he is gone, his beliefs are still alive today. Douglass's words continue to live, showing others the path to freedom and equality for *all* people.

INDEX